# Homework for Heaven

Journaling the Pathway

to Eternal Life

Copyright © 2024 by Monica Hare
All rights reserved.
No portion of this book may be reproduced in any form without written permission from the publisher or author, except as permitted by U.S. copyright law.

All pages in this book are the original work
of Monica Hare unless otherwise attributed.
Design assistance by Cash Hare.
Book Cover by Monica Hare
Email: SearchingForAZebra@outlook.com

Published by Zebra Bunny Publishing
Columbia, Kentucky 42728
https://linktr.ee/searchingforazebra

*Dear Friend,*

Hi! How are you? I don't know if we've ever met, but I want you to know that I have prayed for you. If you have a minute, I'll tell you a little of my story.

I had some things happen in my past (haven't we all?) and I let those bad things give me an excuse to go a little off the rails. But fortunately, God didn't give up on me. He got me going in the right direction, then He blessed me (way more than I deserved). Back then, I didn't go to church, and I didn't read the Bible...but I didn't do anything *bad*. I considered myself a "Christian," but besides saying bedtime prayers with my kids, was I acting like one?

Then one Christmas, I decided I wanted to take my boys to church. My sister picked us up and we went to the little white church. Everyone was friendly, and I thought *maybe we'll go again someday!*

I was surprised when she called the next Saturday and told me she'd pick us up for church on Sunday morning. I agreed to go again—then again and again. After a few weeks of this, I realized *we really should be going on Sunday night, too.* And before long, we were even going on Wednesdays! A few of us started studying the Bible together before Wednesday services...then I got baptized.

I won't lie to you and tell you my life is perfect now (*I* am definitely not perfect). But I will tell you that every time I try to get closer to God, He blesses me more than I deserve. A few months ago I realized, *I am in my 40's and I have never read the whole Bible!* So, I started a Bible plan on my phone and I began reading every morning. Once again, He changed my life.

I started writing every morning after I read the Bible. I would read, pray, then write. (If you haven't read *Searching for a Zebra*, it's on Amazon!) And I would (and do) pray for you. I pray that whoever I come in contact with—whether through a book, online, or in person—be blessed in some way. God knows what you need. If you get closer to Him, He will bless you more than you can imagine.

*Love and prayers,*
*Monica Hare* ♡

# Ready to get started?

~Each page has a verse listed at the top. Open your Bible and look up the verse, then write it on the lines.

~Don't have a Bible nearby? I've added the verses to the back of each page, so you can journal write anytime, anywhere--even if you don't have a Bible in reach.

~As you write the verses, try to remember as much as you can without looking!

~You may want to read the whole chapter (either before or after you write the selected verses). It's important to read *around* the verse to understand the whole context (meaning).

~Use this time to write, pray, and meditate on God's word. It will change your life!

# Romans 5:6-7

*thoughts · questions · connections*

"You see, at just the right time, when we were still powerless, Christ died for the ungodly. Very rarely will anyone die for a righteous person, though for a good person someone might possibly dare to die."
~Romans 5:6-7

# Romans 5:8-9

*thoughts . questions . connections*

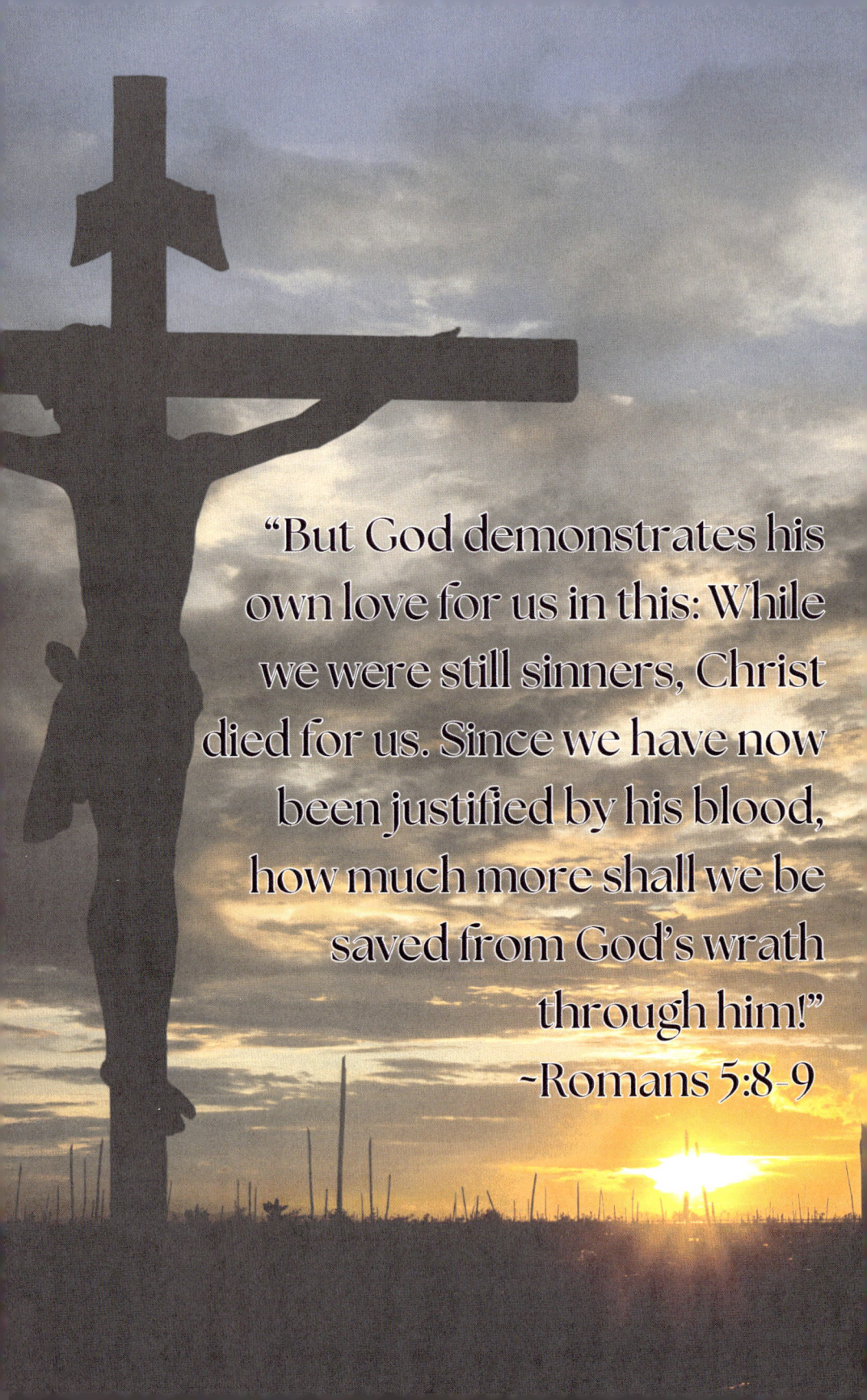

"But God demonstrates his own love for us in this: While we were still sinners, Christ died for us. Since we have now been justified by his blood, how much more shall we be saved from God's wrath through him!"
~Romans 5:8-9

# Ephesians 2:8-9

*thoughts . questions . connections*

For it is by grace you have been saved, through faith—and this is not from yourselves, it is the gift of God—not by works, so that no one can boast.

~Ephesians 2:8-9

# Romans 10:13-15

*thoughts · questions · connections*

for, "Everyone who calls on the name of the Lord will be saved." How, then, can they call on the one they have not believed in? And how can they believe in the one of whom they have not heard? And how can they hear without someone preaching to them? And how can anyone preach unless they are sent? As it is written: "How beautiful are the feet of those who bring good news!"

~Romans 10:13-15

# Acts 16:29-31

*thoughts · questions · connections*

The jailer called for lights, rushed in and fell trembling before Paul and Silas. He then brought them out and asked, "Sirs, what must I do to be saved?" They replied, "Believe in the Lord Jesus, and you will be saved—you and your household."
~Acts 16:29-31

# Acts 16:32-33

*thoughts · questions · connections*

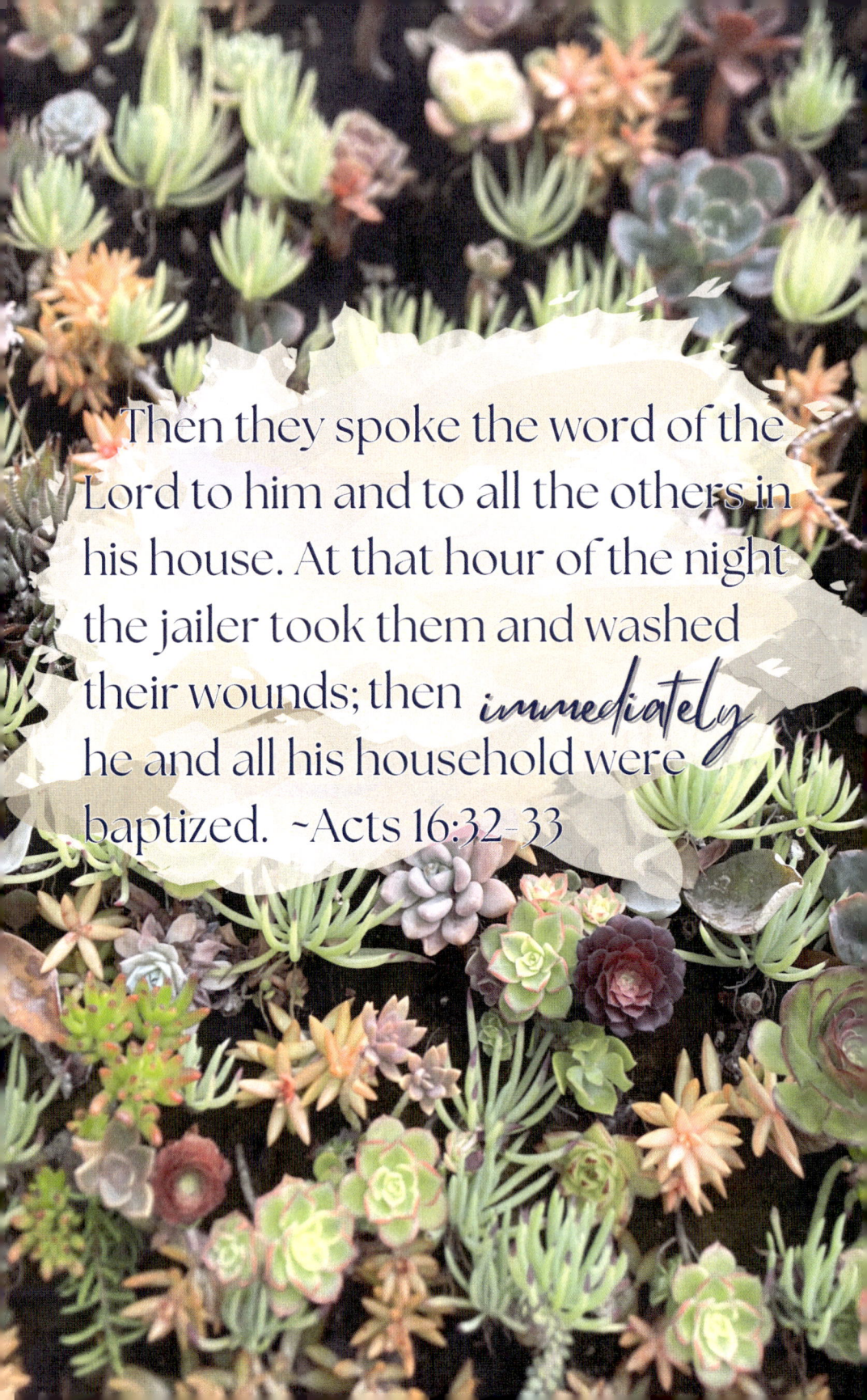

Then they spoke the word of the Lord to him and to all the others in his house. At that hour of the night the jailer took them and washed their wounds; then *immediately* he and all his household were baptized.  ~Acts 16:32-33

# Acts 2:37-38

*thoughts · questions · connections*

When the people heard this, they were cut to the heart and said to Peter and the other apostles, "Brothers, what shall we do?" Peter replied, "Repent and be baptized, every one of you, in the name of Jesus Christ for the forgiveness of your sins. And you will receive the gift of the Holy Spirit."

~Acts 2:37-38

# 1 Peter 3:21-22

*thoughts · questions · connections*

...and this water symbolizes baptism that now saves you also—not the removal of dirt from the body but the pledge of a clear conscience toward God. It saves you by the resurrection of Jesus Christ, who has gone into heaven and is at God's right hand—with angels, authorities and powers in submission to him.
~1 Peter 3:21-22

# Acts 2:39, 41

thoughts · questions · connections

"The promise is for you and your children and for all who are far off —for all whom the Lord our God will call."   ~Acts 2:39

Those who accepted his message were baptized, and about three thousand were added to their number that day.   ~Acts 2:41

# Acts 8:26-28

*thoughts . questions . connections*

Now an angel of the Lord said to Philip, "Go south to the road—the desert road—that goes down from Jerusalem to Gaza." So he started out, and on his way he met an Ethiopia eunuch, an important official in charge of all the treasury of the Kandake (which means "queen of the Ethiopians"). This man had gone to Jerusalem to worship, and on his way home was sitting in his chariot reading the Book of Isaiah the prophet.
~Acts 8:26-28

# Acts 8:36-38

*thoughts . questions . connections*

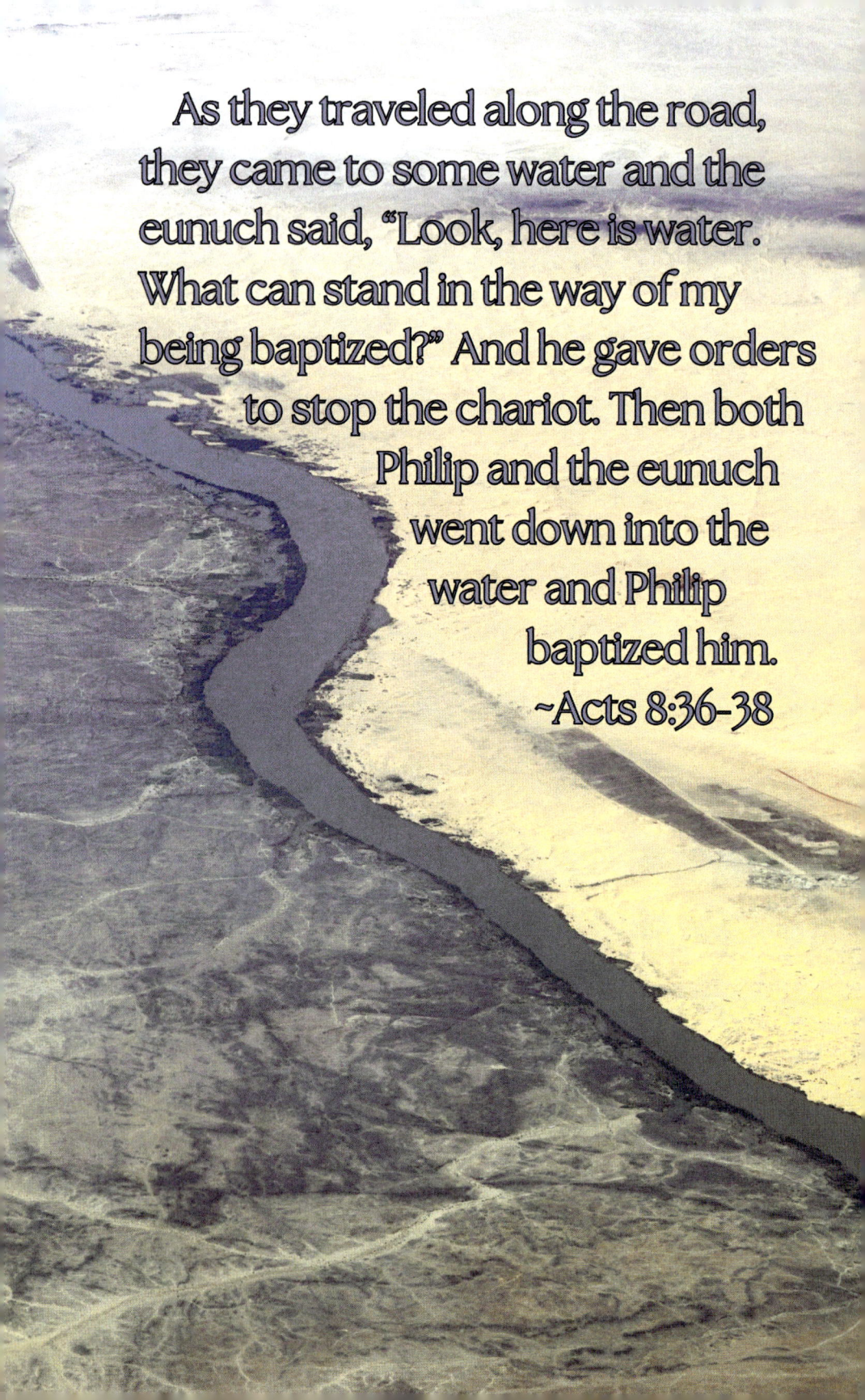

As they traveled along the road, they came to some water and the eunuch said, "Look, here is water. What can stand in the way of my being baptized?" And he gave orders to stop the chariot. Then both Philip and the eunuch went down into the water and Philip baptized him.
~Acts 8:36-38

# Romans 10:9-10

*thoughts . questions . connections*

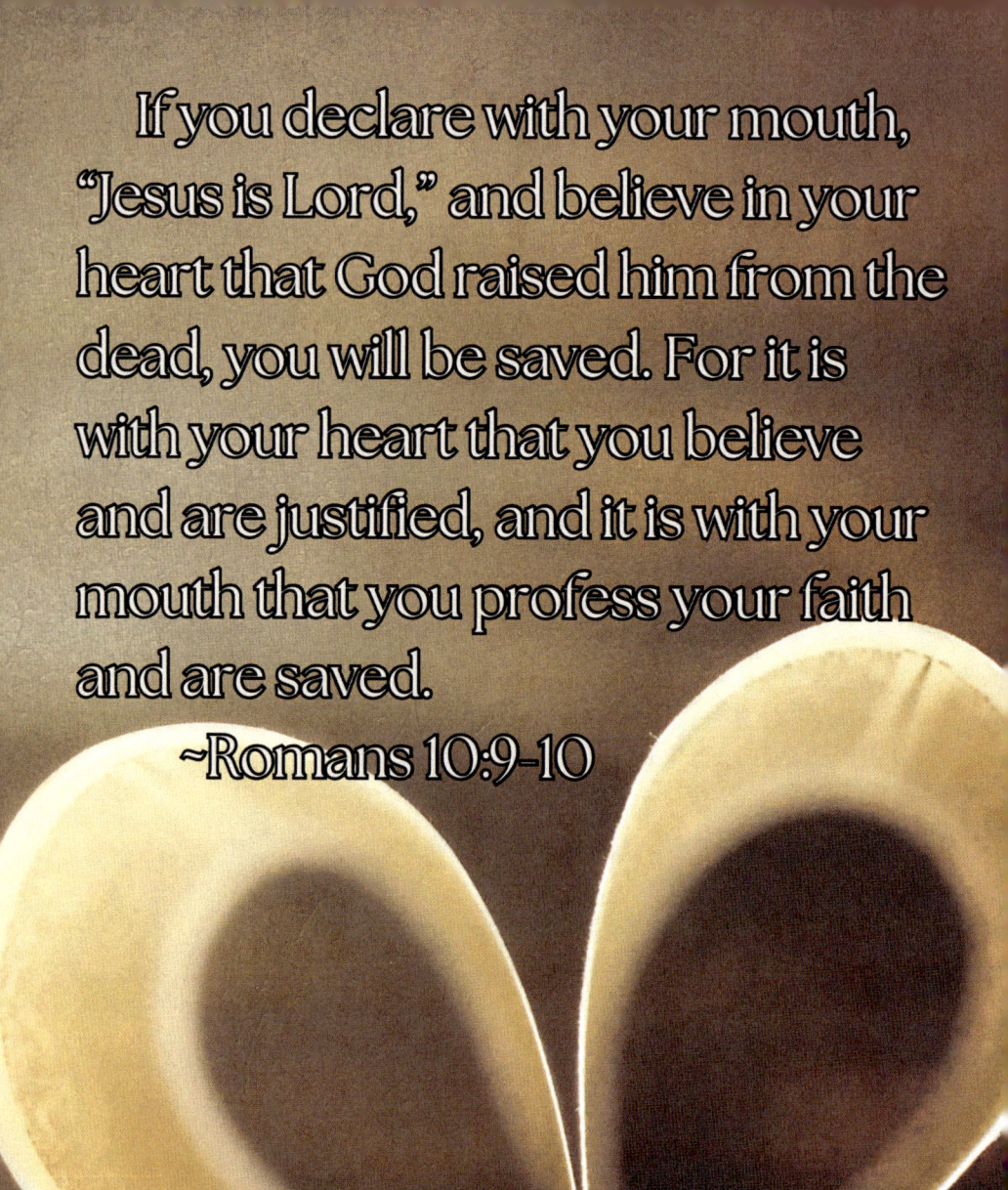

If you declare with your mouth, "Jesus is Lord," and believe in your heart that God raised him from the dead, you will be saved. For it is with your heart that you believe and are justified, and it is with your mouth that you profess your faith and are saved.
~Romans 10:9-10

# Hebrews 11:1

# Hebrews 11:3

*thoughts . questions . connections*

Now faith is confidence in what we hope for and assurance about what we do not see.
~Hebrews 11:1.

By faith we understand that the universe was formed at God's command, so that what is seen was not made out of what was visible.
~Hebrews 11:3

# James 2:14-17

*thoughts · questions · connections*

What good is it, my brothers and sisters, if someone claims to have faith but has no deeds? Can such faith save them? Suppose a brother or a sister is without clothes and daily food. If one of you says to them,

"Go in peace; keep warm and well fed,"

but does *nothing* about their physical needs, what good is it? In the same way, faith by itself, if it is not accompanied by action, is dead.

~James 2: 14-17

# Mark 16:15-16

# Acts 4:12

*thoughts · questions · connections*

He said to them, "Go into all the world and preach the gospel to all creation. Whoever believes and is baptized will be saved, but whoever does not believe will be condemned.
~Mark 16:15-16

Salvation is found in no one else, for there is no other name under heaven given to mankind by which we must be saved."
~Acts 4:12

# Romans 6:3-5

*thoughts . questions . connections*

"Or don't you know that all of us who were baptized into Christ Jesus were baptized into his death? We were therefore buried with him through baptism into death in order that, just as Christ was raised from the dead through the glory of the Father, we too may live a new life. For if we have been united with him in a death like his, we will certainly also be united with him in a resurrection like his."

~Romans 6:3-5

# Matthew 10:30-33

*thoughts . questions . connections*

And even the very hairs of your head are all numbered. So don't be afraid; you are worth more than many sparrows. "Whoever acknowledges me before others, I will also acknowledge before my Father in heaven. But whoever disowns me before others, I will disown before my Father in heaven.
~Matthew 10:30-33

# Hebrews 13:6-8

*thoughts . questions . connections*

So we say with confidence, "The Lord is my helper; I will not be afraid. What can mere mortals do to me?" Remember your leaders, who spoke the word of God to you. Consider the outcome of their way of life and imitate their faith. Jesus Christ is the same yesterday and today and forever.
~Hebrews 13:6-8

# Galatians 3:26-27

# Ephesians 4:4-6

*thoughts · questions · connections*

So in Christ Jesus you are all children of God through faith, for all of you who were baptized into Christ have clothed yourselves with Christ.
~Galatians 3:26-27

"There is one body and one Spirit, just as you were called to one hope when you were called; one Lord, one faith, one baptism; one God and Father of all, who is over all and through all and in all."
~Ephesians 4:4-6

# Romans 8:38-39

*thoughts . questions . connections*

For I am convinced that neither death nor life, neither angels nor demons, neither the present nor the future, nor any powers, neither height nor depth, nor anything else in all creation, will be able to separate us from the love of God that is in Christ Jesus our Lord.
~Romans 8:38-39

# Why write the Bible?

### • To remember!

You are much more likely to remember content you generate (write) rather than something you only read. What better way to *write them on the tablet of your heart?*

### • It's good for your brain!

Studies have shown that when you write, your brain has higher levels of electrical activity across areas associated with memory, vision, and processing.

### • Handwriting is fun!

Buy yourself some pretty pens, find a quiet place, and make this journal yours.

### • Relax!

Copying the Bible is peaceful. You can feel confident that you are doing the absolute best thing you can be doing at that time, while focusing on the word of God--and clearing your mind of distractions.

Connect with me at:

Made in United States
Orlando, FL
22 September 2024